# Real Repertoire
# *Piano Duets*
## grades 4–6

### Selected and edited by Christine Brown

FABER ﬀ MUSIC

## EDITOR'S NOTE

The keyboard duet as a form of chamber music gained in importance as the piano developed from its predecessors, the virginal, clavichord and harpsichord. The limited range of the earlier instruments and the physical difficulty of seating two performers (especially ladies in wide skirts) at the small keyboards slowed down the early development of the medium, but by 1765 Mozart's Piano Sonata in C, K.19d had been published and the mature Mozart was writing works which surpassed any previous duets.

It is not surprising that many famous teachers in the past advocated piano duets for their pupils. Schubert wrote some of his finest piano duets for his pupils, the two daughters of Count Esterhazy, and Beethoven requested that Czerny, to whom he had entrusted his nephew Karl's musical education, should give the boy more piano duets.

There are various considerations to be addressed when playing duets. The problem of positioning two adult players at one keyboard can be eased if they sit on separate stools set at a slight angle. It is then possible for the fingers of Secondo's right hand to play over or under those of Primo's left hand (and vice versa). The choice of which player is to pedal must also be solved. As pedalling is to a large extent dependent on harmony, it is usually better for Secondo to operate both pedals because temporary changes may cause confusion. In chamber music there must be a leader and the leading must be done clearly and sensitively. A whispered count of a preliminary bar or a small movement of head or finger will usually be sufficient.

Although the piano duet is perhaps the strangest form of chamber music in that the two players perform on just one instrument, playing piano duets will bring hours of pleasure to performers and listeners alike.

*Christine Brown*

## THE COMPOSERS AND THEIR DUETS

WOLFGANG AMADEUS MOZART (1756–1791) was born in Salzburg and died in Vienna. As a small child, Mozart wrote a three movement *Sonata in C*, K.19d, which he performed with his sister on a harpsichord and which his father later declared to be the first published piano duet. The mature Mozart recognized the potential for the medium as the range of the instrument increased and its resonance became greater, so his later sonatas for piano duet had a richer texture than his solo piano sonatas. The beautiful *Andante* from the *Sonata in D*, K.381 was written in Salzburg in about 1772 and is in modified sonata form, the two players sharing both melodic and harmonic interest. Indeed in the central section the players imitate one another before the return of the recapitulation and the brief coda.

LUDWIG VAN BEETHOVEN (1770–1827) was born in Bonn and died in Vienna. The *Sonata in D* for piano duet Op.6 was published in 1797 at the same time as the important solo sonata in E flat Op.7. It shows some similarities with the music of his Viennese contemporaries. The arresting, strongly masculine opening is followed by a gentle second subject which provides opportunities for lyrical playing. Take the 'Allegro molto' literally. Try counting aloud three in a bar at first, then try feeling one in a bar.

CARL MARIA VON WEBER (1786–1826) was born in Eutin and died in London. He was a composer, conductor, critic and one of the most brilliant pianists of his generation. He wrote three sets of piano duets. The first set, written in 1801 when he was only 14, includes the exciting *Sonatina* which provides valuable and enjoyable ensemble opportunities.

ANTON DIABELLI (1781–1858) was born near Salzburg and died in Vienna after a successful career as a music publisher, editor and composer. He is perhaps most famous for writing the waltz on which Beethoven wrote thirty-three variations, but his own output was large and included masses, songs and a large number of piano pieces. Among these were the *Melodious Exercises* for piano duet, Op.149, which provide an ideal introduction to four-hand playing.

JOHANNES BRAHMS (1833–1897) was born in Hamburg, where he spent his childhood, and died in Vienna. He travelled widely, met Joachim, Liszt and Schumann and wrote many large-scale works for orchestra, much choral and chamber music and a substantial amount of piano music. On one of his visits to Vienna, where he eventually settled, he composed a set of sixteen waltzes for piano duet which he also arranged for piano solo. The fifteenth waltz is in A major in the duet version, but in A flat in the solo version.

GABRIEL FAURÉ (1845–1924) was born in Pamiers and died in Paris. He was trained as a church musician at the École Niedermeyer. A gifted pianist and organist, his compositions for these instruments have earned a permanent place in the repertoire. The suite for piano duet was written for Hélène (nicknamed Dolly) who was the daughter of his friend, the soprano Emma Bardac. The tender *Berceuse*, which suggests the little girl rocking her doll to sleep, provides the perfect introduction to Fauré's lyrical style.

OTTORINO RESPIGHI (1879–1936) was born in Bologna and died in Rome where he had taught at the Liceo de Santa Cecilia. He is most famous for his richly-scored orchestral tone-poems, but his *Six Little Pieces* for piano duet, written in 1926, is a charming and valuable addition to the piano duet repertoire. The first piece, a delightfully sentimental *Romance*, requires good balance, careful coordination between the players and some skilful pedalling from Secondo.

CÉCILE LOUISE STÉPHANIE CHAMINADE (1857–1944) was born in Paris and died in Monte Carlo. She studied at first with her mother, then with Félix Le Couppey and Benjamin Godard. When only seven years old, she played some of her compositions to Bizet, who was very impressed. Although she wrote orchestral works, a piano concerto and much chamber music, she is best remembered for her popular salon pieces for the piano. The charming *Pastorale* for piano duet gives equal opportunities to both players.

ALEC ROWLEY (1892–1958) was born and died in London. He studied at the Royal Academy of Music where he won many important prizes. Later he taught at Trinity College and became well-known as a teacher, writer, composer and pianist. As a performer he particularly enjoyed playing piano duets with Edgar Moy and they frequently broadcast together. He wrote a large quantity of piano music including some delightful duets which skilfully allow equal interest to both players.

MÁTYÁS SEIBER (1905–1960) was born in Budapest and died in South Africa. He studied at the Budapest Academy with Adolf Shiffer for the cello and Kodály for composition. His interest in jazz is shown in many of his works including the two volumes of *Easy Dances* for piano. The volume for piano duet includes a *Ragtime* and a *Blues* as well as the more traditional dances such as a *Waltz* and a *Foxtrot*. *Tango Argentino* requires loose wrists for the rapid thirds in the Primo part and accurate timing from both players.

# SECONDO
# ANDANTE
from Sonata in D, K.381

Wolfgang Amadeus Mozart
(1756–1791)

© 2009 by Faber Music Ltd.

PRIMO

# ANDANTE

from Sonata in D, K.381

Wolfgang Amadeus Mozart
(1756–1791)

# SECONDO
# ALLEGRO MOLTO

from Sonata in D, Op.6

Ludwig van Beethoven
(1770–1827)

V. S.

PRIMO
# ALLEGRO MOLTO
from Sonata in D, Op.6

Ludwig van Beethoven
(1770–1827)

V. S.

V. S.

SECONDO

# SONATINA

Op.3, No.1

Carl Maria von Weber
(1786–1826)

# SONATINA
Op.3, No.1

Carl Maria von Weber
(1786–1826)

SECONDO

# POLONAISE IN A

Op.149, No.23

Anton Diabelli
(1781–1858)

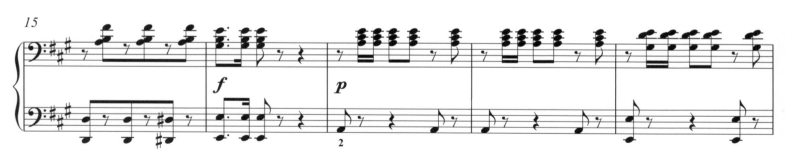

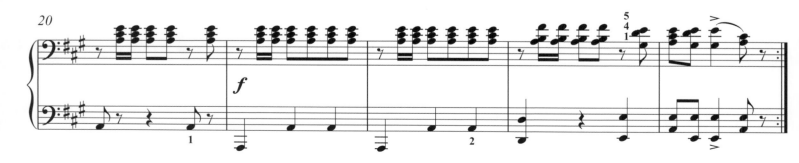

# POLONAISE IN A

Op.149, No.23

Anton Diabelli
(1781–1858)

SECONDO
# ALLEGRO IN E MINOR
Op.149, No.28

Anton Diabelli
(1781–1858)

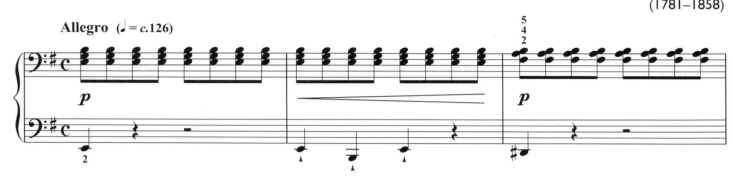

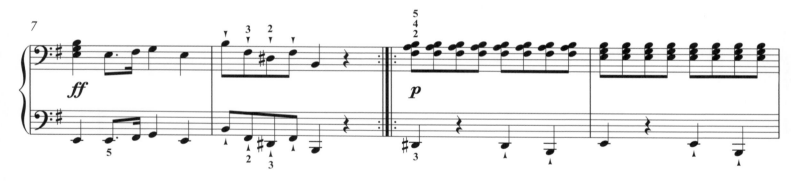

# ALLEGRO IN E MINOR

Op.149, No.28

Anton Diabelli
(1781–1858)

# SECONDO
# WALTZ IN A

Op.39, No.15

Johannes Brahms
(1833–1897)

PRIMO
# WALTZ IN A
Op.39, No.15

Johannes Brahms
(1833–1897)

SECONDO
# BERCEUSE
from Dolly Suite Op.56, No.1

Gabriel Fauré
(1845–1924)

\* The bracket indicates that this note should be omitted when playing with a partner.

PRIMO
# BERCEUSE
from Dolly Suite Op.56, No.1

Gabriel Fauré
(1845–1924)

Allegretto moderato ( ♩ = c.60 )

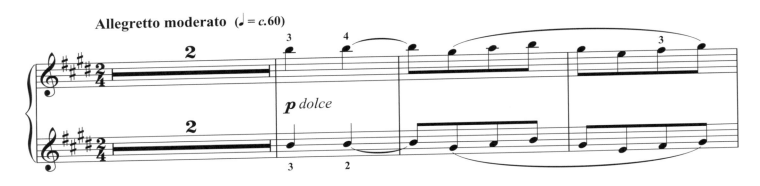

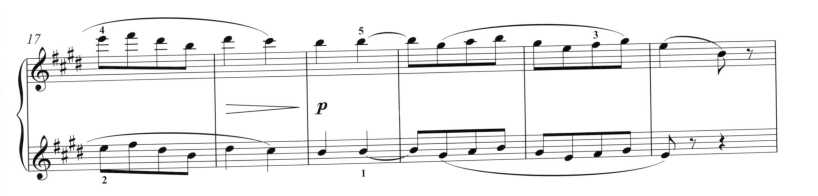

SECONDO

# ROMANCE

from Six Little Pieces

Ottorino Respighi
(1879–1936)

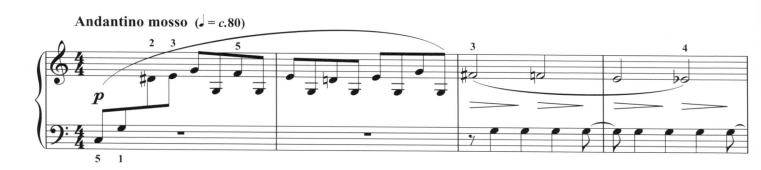

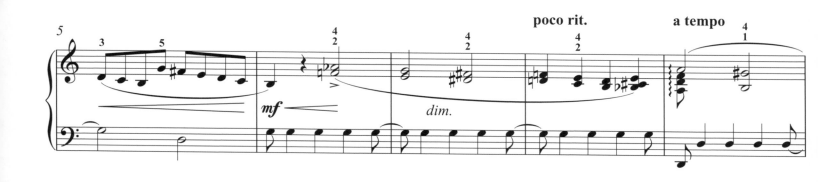

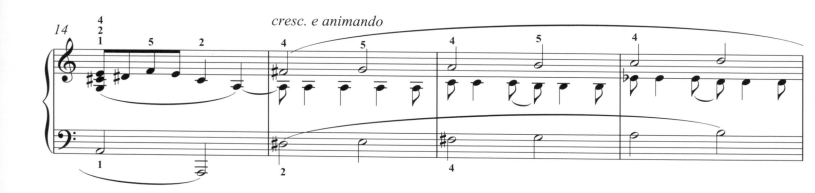

PRIMO
# ROMANCE
from Six Little Pieces

Ottorino Respighi
(1879–1936)

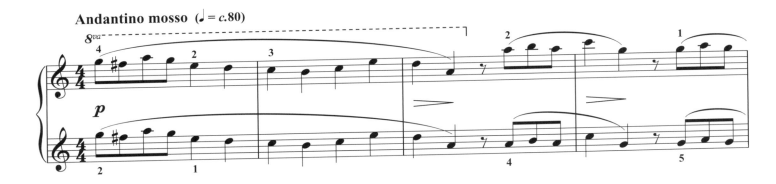

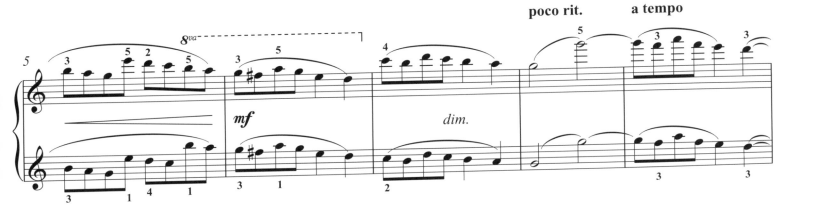

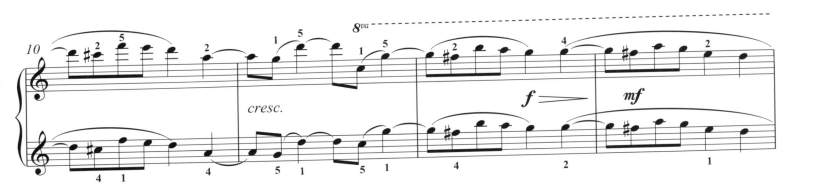

* Play the octave with 1-5, put down the sustaining pedal then change
from 1 to 5 on the higher A and keep it down throughout the bar.

SECONDO
# PASTORALE

Cécile Chaminade
(1857–1944)

PRIMO
# PASTORALE

Cécile Chaminade
(1857–1944)

SECONDO

# BADINAGE

Alec Rowley
(1892–1958)

# BADINAGE

Alec Rowley
(1892–1958)

SECONDO
# TANGO ARGENTINO

Matyas Seiber
(1905–1960)

PRIMO
# TANGO ARGENTINO

Matyas Seiber
(1905–1960)

© 2009 by Faber Music Ltd
This edition first published in 2009
Bloomsbury House 74–77 Great Russell Street London WC1B 3DA
Music processed by Jackie Leigh
Cover design by Sue Clarke
Printed in England by Caligraving Ltd

ISBN10: 0-571-53140-7
EAN13: 978-0-571-53140-0

To buy Faber Music or Trinity publications or to find out about the full range of titles
available please contact your local music retailer or Faber Music sales enquiries:

Faber Music Ltd, Burnt Mill, Elizabeth Way, Harlow CM20 2HX
Tel: +44 (0)1279 82 89 82   Fax: +44 (0)1279 82 89 83
sales@fabermusic.com   fabermusic.com